HOW DO YOU KNOW THAT?

HOW DO YOU KNOW THAT?

ELLIS POTTER

Destinée Media

Published by: Destinée Media
www.destineemedia.com

Chief editor: Peco Gaskovski
Photo of the author: Andrea Peterson

This book is dedicated to
www.labri.org
where many of the ideas in it began

■   ■   ■   ■

How do you know that?

When I asked this question as a child, I was told, 'You'll understand when you are older', or 'The Trinity is a paradox', or given some other vague response. It was frustrating to hear that kind of response. It didn't help me to trust the people I was asking. Much of my life has been a search for ways to answer *How do you know that?*—and to safely push the envelope of knowing. This book is the result of 67 years (so far) of pushing.

Like most people, you have probably asked *How do you know that?* many times in your life. How old were you when you first asked it? How old were you when someone first asked *you*? Many children start asking it at two or three years of age.

'How do you know that?' includes 'Who told you?' and 'What is your source for knowing it?' We all need to be secure about what we know. Different sources of knowledge are often in conflict or competition with each other in our lives and societies. Is this the way it should be?

Our identity and the meaning of our lives depend upon how we know. It can be confusing and stressful when different sources of knowledge are in competition with each other. How can we deal with this? Should we pick one source and reject the other? Should we free ourselves of authoritative sources of knowledge altogether?

In this book, we will explore some authoritative sources that inform our knowledge. In some ways, these sources are quite different from each other; in fact, they might seem as if they don't go together at all, or will compete with each other. But what if the different sources of authority actually *complete* or 'complement' each other? We will explore this possibility, in order to see how it may give us a richer and fuller understanding of our lives and the world.

WHAT ARE AUTHORITIES?

What are the authorities in your life? When I pose this question to groups of people, I usually get a long and unpredictable list of answers. Here is a sample:

Parents
God
Police
Government
Teachers
Peers
Friends
Myself
The Law
Gravity
Celebrities
Experience
Media
Advertisers
Food
Family
Nation
Mental Faculties
Senses
Science
Moral Values
Pastor
Encyclopedia
Bible
Feelings
Weather
The Devil

What do all of these examples of authority have in common? In other words, what *is* authority? Some people say 'influence'. Others say, 'a source of truth'. Many people say, 'Authority is something that you give to someone or something', although that doesn't seem to work. For instance, you can't 'give' authority to gravity, because gravity just has it. Some things and some people have authority whether we give it or not. They have authority before we were born. The idea that authority is inherent in some things does not mean that the authority is friendly or convenient to us. If you fall off a building, gravity won't cooperate to save your life.

Often people think of authority as 'power'. But they don't mean something like electricity; they are talking about power in human relationships. Authority seems to include both personal and impersonal aspects. Most people also realize that authority is necessary for life, although it can be misused or misapplied. If I were to put it in my own words, I would define authority like this:

Authority is the power to describe reality.

How can we understand this? How can we apply this to real life? Think of parents and children. Parents are an authority for young children, because parents have the power to describe reality for children. They describe bedtime, playtime, and diet for children. They describe where children can play—in the backyard or in the garden, but not in the busy street.

Very young children cannot describe reality for themselves and need the authority of their parents for survival. They don't have the necessary vision or the scope of experience. Their lives depend on the authority of their parents. They may die if they play in the street rather than in the garden.

We also know that parents don't always exercise authority perfectly. During childhood we were all, to some extent, distorted and wounded and squashed by our fathers and mothers, because they made mistakes in exercising their authority. Still, insofar as children cannot describe reality for themselves, they must depend on their parents. There's no way around it.

It isn't only little children who need authority. People of all ages need the authority of the law and government and society and family and economic structures, in order to be safe from chaos and death.

Doctors are another example of authority. A doctor has the power to describe illness and health to the patient. A doctor can say, 'This is your disease, this is why you are sick, and here is the medication you need to cure the sickness.' In many cases a patient will die if they refuse the authority of the doctor. And just as there are imperfect parents, there are imperfect doctors. Sometimes you get a doctor who is incompetent, in which case his authority may be unhelpful and even dangerous. Occasionally, a doctor may only prescribe medication X, because he knows that the company that manufactures medication

X will reward him with a luxurious holiday if he sells enough bottles of X.

As you can see by these examples of human authority, there is no guarantee that the authority will *describe* reality accurately. The authority simply describes it. We hope that the description is accurate, but sometimes it isn't. There's an element of trust in living with authority. Trusting means taking a risk and believing there will be a benefit to a relationship of authority, rather than harm. Interpersonal authority functions best when there is trust.

Advertisers have the authority to describe the reality of pleasure and beauty and health to the public. They have the power to tell us how to identify ourselves: how to be acceptable, and wanted, and envied, and influential, and admired. Advertisers have the power to convince us that buying and using a variety of products will give us a good identity and fulfillment.

Authority is connected with the word 'auto', which means 'self', as in 'automobile' and 'autobiography'. But if authority is related to the 'self', which self should we start with? Should we start with 'myself'? Does that mean I have to be a God for myself? Am I good at being God? Or might 'self' refer to a powerful other self, or a trusted other self? Should the other self be God?

Here is another question involving the 'auto' of authority: What do we call a person who writes a book? We call him an 'author'. An author has the authority to describe the reality in the book.

If Mary writes a novel, she might write, 'John is an alcoholic.' When George reads the book, he might say, 'I don't think John is an alcoholic. It's not fair or nice to call John an alcoholic.' How do you think Mary will respond? If she is like most authors, then she'll probably say, 'My dear George, you're completely crazy because I am the author of my book and I can say whatever I want. If I say that John is green with five legs, then he's green with five legs. To this book I am God.' That's an author's authority. The author of a book has the power to describe the reality in the book however he or she wants.

The way people use authority can be good or bad or smart or stupid, a blessing or a curse, but in each case it involves the power to describe what the world is like.

There are many kinds of authority in the world. The focus of this book is the authoritative sources that inform our knowledge—our knowledge about anything. What has authority to help us to *know truly*?

EPISTEMOLOGY IS NOT A DISEASE

What is *epistemology*? It's not a disease. It's the study of how we know, and how we know we know. Epistemology has its roots in the Greek words for 'knowledge' and 'study of', so it's about how we comprehend and contextualize our information. It's about how we process and relate to information and experiences.

Epistemology is a very ordinary thing. It happens every day, and in quite different ways. For example, do you know that you like chocolate? If you do, then how do you know that? Do you have to discuss it with somebody before you know you like it? Do you have to read a book to figure out that you like it? Do you have to work out a mathematical equation to know that you like it?

No. You know that you like it by experience. You put the chocolate in your mouth, and you experience pleasure, and you know. This knowledge is not open to discussion. If you tell me, 'I like chocolate', and if I doubt that, then I'm being silly.

The Romans had a proverb: 'De gustibus non est disputandum.' This means, 'Taste is not debatable.' It is rooted in experience. Similarly, if you tell me that your favorite color is red, it's ridiculous for me to say, 'That is wrong, it should be blue', or to say, 'Don't you want to change it to blue?' Experience cannot be disputed, although the meaning of it can.

How about this: Do you know that two plus two equals four? How do you know that? Some people say that their teacher once told them that two plus two equals four. But the teacher could not have told them all the combinations of numbers that could be added. We learn a rational process of knowing how numbers combine and fit together. Rational means experiencing reality in 'ratios', which are relationships.

You know that two plus two equals four, but you don't know what it tastes like. So your knowledge of two plus two is different from your knowledge of chocolate. Which is the more true knowledge? They are equally true, but very different.

Do you know that you stop at the red light and go at the green light? How do you know that? Many people say that that knowledge is logical. But it isn't. Red is a hot, active color, and it means 'go'. Ask any bull or bee. Green is a cool, quiet color. It means rest. Ask any interior decorator. Our knowledge about the red light and the green light is not logical; it is traditional or cultural. It is true, necessary and life-saving knowledge. Even if this knowledge is not rational, it wouldn't be wise to ignore it. We need this kind of knowledge in order to live our lives. It is a deeply set custom and rhythm for our lives. That red means stop and green means go has become a given for pedestrians and motor vehicle drivers. We might get into an accident and die if we disregarded it. Cultural and traditional knowledge is different from experiential and rational knowledge, but equally true.

Do you know that your friend likes you? How do you know that? Perhaps they tell you. Maybe they don't avoid you. They might laugh at your jokes and try to encourage you. This knowledge can be subtle, but it can also be very strong. We need this kind of knowledge in our lives.

Do you know that the Bible, or Koran, or Upanishads, or Torah, or some other holy book, is true? How do you know that? You might know it because of its historical veracity, or its internal consistency, or its healthy application to your own life. Your knowledge that the Bible or another holy book is true is also going to include faith—in a similar way that you need a degree of faith to know that your friend likes you.

As you can see by these examples, there are many different ways of knowing. Are there other examples that you can think of? Knowing is rich and complex—so much so that we cannot have a total controlling grasp of knowing. We cannot see the whole picture from the point of view of any one way of knowing. We don't know what everything tastes like, and not everything has a taste; and not all of our knowledge is logical. And yet the different ways of knowing belong together in a full and lively epistemology. The relationship between these different kinds of knowing should not be competition, but complementarity. That means that they need and complete each other.

The Four Corners

Now let's look at the different *sources* that inform our knowing. To begin with, imagine a square. Each of the corners will represent an authoritative source that informs our knowledge or epistemology.

We'll explore each of these corners individually, as well as their relationship to each other, and see why all of them are needed for a full epistemology.

THE FIRST CORNER

The first corner is labelled **B** for **Bible** (or Revelation). The Bible, or other revelations like the Koran, Upanishads, and Vedas, tell us things about reality that we could not know in any other way. For instance, the Bible tells us that reality is not mechanical, but fundamentally personal, beginning with a God who is a Trinity of three Persons. This information, if true, could not be determined by science or rationality. It could not be discovered by observation of the physical world or by laboratory experimentation. It is revelatory knowledge. Of course, such information should not conflict with science or rationality; it should complement what we learn on the basis of science and rationality. But the information itself cannot be obtained scientifically.

Revelation means information that comes from the supernatural into the natural world. As an example, consider information itself. It is widely understood, especially in the field of biology, that information (i.e., the genetic code) governs the functioning of the material of life. Although information obviously exists and controls matter, there is no evidence that matter *produces* information. In trying to understand this, the most reasonable hypothesis or assumption is that information is supernatural. The more religious hypothesis is that matter *does* produce information, and we have faith that the process will eventually be discovered. The religion of this hypothesis is 'scientism', or the belief that science can discover all truth (based on the unproven assumption that matter comprises all of reality). But this kind of faith seems rather extreme. Science is a wonderful gift, but worshipping it is not a good idea.

THE SECOND CORNER

The second corner is labelled **R** for **Rationality**. As I mentioned earlier, rationality means seeing reality in ratios, or relationships. Understanding ratios or relationships involves logic; such understanding can generally be expressed mathematically.

We learn things about reality from our rationality that we cannot learn from the Bible or other revelations. For instance, as a result of rationality, dental science has developed. The Bible makes no mention of dentistry. Someone who wants their knowledge to be informed only by the Bible (or the Revelation corner in general) might not ever go to the dentist, because dentistry is extra-biblical knowledge. However, knowledge of dentistry is one way of obeying the biblical command to have dominion over creation. We should not 'go with the flow' of tooth decay, but have dominion over it. In this way, dentistry is not in conflict with what we learn from the Bible, but is in a complementary (or completing) relationship with the Bible. It brings us a more full understanding of the world.

Rationality also gives people dominion over the rest of creation. Civilization requires the manipulation of nature, according to the rational imagination of people. For example, wheat naturally grows along stream banks, mixed with many other plants. Human civilization requires human beings to say to the wheat, 'You will grow only in this field, and no other plants will grow here.' This is not how wheat naturally behaves. This happens because a supernatural source of rational, imaginative, and creative power, is imposed on the wheat. If human beings did not manipulate nature in this rational and creative way, then society would never be possible. We would have to go back to living as hunters and gatherers. At the same time, this domination of nature must include careful husbandry and preservation, or there won't be any nature left to work with.

If the relationship between rationality and revelation is complementary, it means both corners are essential and neither corner is adequate. There are also ways in which they interrelate. If God has created the world, then we can find out many things about the Creator by examining the creation. The creation is beautiful, orderly, faithful, and dependable; and God invites us to observe all of this, to better understand Him. The more we discover through archeology, molecular biology, quantum physics, and other disciplines that depend upon reason, the more we know about God and His work.

THE THIRD CORNER

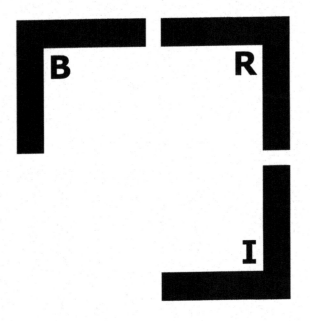

The lower right corner **I** represents **Institution**, or tradition, the third authoritative source that informs our knowledge.

Institution means various groups of people living together over time. It includes marriage, family, friendship, community, nation, church, and other situations where people are in relationship with each other. All institutions develop traditions, which help us to build and preserve our knowledge, so that each generation does not need to reinvent the wheel. Some traditions are short-lived and others last longer.

We learn things from institutions that we don't learn from rationality or by revelation. Knowledge gained through institution cannot be expressed mathematically. Institution brings us knowledge through relationships between people.

The revelation of the Bible (e.g., 1 John 4:19-21) tells us that we can only know God and His love by loving each other. We can only love each other in institutions. We cannot know this love by doing a religious ceremony. We cannot know it by just feeling it either. Love is not a feeling. Love is a series of responsible choices that promote and encourage the other so that they can become who God intends them to be. The purpose of love is to make us more fully real. As you can see, love is not self-centered. The center of love, the focus of love, is the other person. So the purpose of love is not to express my satisfaction or my desire or my enjoyment. The purpose of love is not to gratify myself, or even to gratify the other. The purpose of love is to establish people in truth. For this reason, love can sometimes be experienced as difficult or painful.

Many people feel that they know the love of God when they experience people loving them. This is half of the truth. This is love that we receive, or get. The other half of the truth is that we know the love of God by loving other people sacrificially. This is the love that we do. The relationship between getting and doing should be complementary rather than competitive.

We cannot know love only by reading the Bible. We cannot know love by reason. We have to live out this love in relationships, in institutions. In the Old Testament, the Hebrew word for 'know' means sexual intercourse. That's not something you do rationally at a distance. It's a committed, engaged, involved way of knowing.

We should not think that we can go and live in a cave with our Bible and know God in all the ways we need to. It doesn't work like that in the biblical worldview. The Bible tells us that we need to live in relationships, families, churches, cultures, and nations. Knowing God includes loving others within these institutions.

Of course, knowing by and through the institution or tradition can be exaggerated or confused. Sometimes people say, 'We know this is true because we have always done it this way.' Or, 'This is true because we have always believed it.' Or, an elderly church member who is disturbed by modern translations of the Bible may say, 'If the King James version was good enough for the apostle Paul, it is good enough for me.' This kind of thinking removes the corner **I** from the necessary context of the other corners.

Our understanding of the Christian faith was deepened through the various early church councils and historical developments within the church. These institutions gave us increasing definition and refinement of the truth as expressed in the Bible. An example of this refinement is the Nicene Creed, which begins like this: 'We believe in one God, the Father Almighty, Maker of heaven and earth, and of all things visible and invisible. And in one Lord Jesus Christ, the only-begotten Son of God....'

There is nothing in the Nicene Creed that you won't find in the Bible. The Creed was developed by a group of people who gathered and wanted to find a way to express key ideas from the Bible. The Creed is a product of that gathering, of those people who came together in prayer and conversation and Scripture reading. The Creed adds definition and refinement to our understanding of God and the Christian faith. It focuses believers on central aspects of the truth, while also preventing heresies from entering into people's understanding of God. The Creed doesn't alter anything that the Bible says—it doesn't reinvent the wheel, doesn't reinvent the truth—but reflects and distills the truth.

The Nicene Creed is an example of knowledge that comes to us through community or institutions. We know about God by living in the historical institution of the church. We know by the giving, submitting, and mutually supportive relationships of the community of His people.

Many of us have suffered in churches from bad leaders, prejudice, bigotry, abuse, rejection, manipulation, or tyranny. We might be tempted to eliminate the church because of these problems; but that would be like throwing out the proverbial baby with the bathwater. The institution needs to be part of the mix of how we live in reality and know reality.

There is another, deeper way of seeing the importance of relationships in epistemology. It is the realization that fact does not equal truth. Truth is fact plus meaning. What does meaning mean? Meaning means relationships, which means that nothing has meaning in itself. For instance, the meaning of the color red is not in the color red. It is in its relationships with green, and blue, and other colors. The meaning of Adam in the creation account of the Bible was not in himself but in his relationships with God and with Eve. The meaning of Jesus is not in Jesus but in his relationship with the Father and the Holy Spirit. The meaning of you is not in you but in your relationships with others. All true knowledge is relational in a variety of ways.

THE FOURTH CORNER

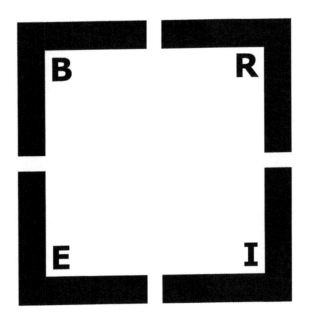

The fourth corner **E** stands for **Experience**. Our personal experience is essential for understanding reality. We need to experience awe, fear, sorrow, hope, comfort, and thankfulness because we don't get them from the other corners. Personal experiences are subjective, meaning that they depend upon your point of view, which is unique. But the fact that they are subjective does not mean that they are untrue. There are objective and subjective parts of truth, which are both essential. Actually, we find that there is no objective truth, and there is no subjective truth. All true truth is always both objective and subjective. The true and lively relationship between the objectivity and subjectivity of truth should be complementary rather than competitive.

If four people witness an automobile accident from different vantage points, what they see, or subjectively experience, is going to be different from each other. Their experiences of the accident should not compete with each other but complement each other to give a truer knowledge of what happened. Some literary critics of the Four Gospels would want us to believe that because there is not only one objective experience of the accident but several subjective experiences, the accident never happened. The accident happened, and Jesus objectively happened. There are subjective views of both.

Personal experience is an authoritative source of knowledge about reality. We each have individual, subjective, 'unshareable' experiences of nature, humanness, love, healing, knowledge, guidance, imagination, intuition, and reality as a whole. All of these experiences inform our epistemology. We learn things through those personal experiences that we don't learn through reading the Bible. We don't learn those things by thinking and reasoning. We don't learn them from institutions.

Christians know that God loves them because He comforts them. He thrills them. He gives them joy and fills their hearts with wonder and the Holy Spirit. God is a personal and relational God, and so a person's knowledge of God cannot be at a distance. It must be very intimate. It will be unique for each person. It's like a marriage: I could not share the deep experiences of my marriage with you, any more than you could share your experience of marriage with me. And yet the experience is essential for us to truly know marriage.

However, although experience is necessary, it can't be isolated from the other corners. If I depend only on my experience to know reality, I'm living in an experience bubble. In that case, I would need to say, 'God *is* my experience.' But if God isn't more than my experience, then I am worshipping myself, which is totally self-referential. This is not Christianity. It is humanism or self-ism; it forces you to be your own God.

GETTING SQUARE

Each of the four corners is a different authority for our knowledge of reality. Each corner is *unique*, in the sense that it tells us something that the other corners cannot. Each corner is *essential*, in the sense that we cannot understand God and the whole of reality if we leave any of the corners out of the epistemology.

We need all four corners. We cannot know reality truly if we only have our rationality. We cannot know reality truly if we only have the authority and tradition of the community. We cannot know reality truly if we sit in a room and read a holy book all day. If we have only personal experience, and we see angels and make prophecies, but don't have the other corners to complete our understanding of reality, then our personal experience is not enough—and may even be dangerous.

In fact, all of the corners, if isolated, can be dangerous. But that does not mean we can live without them. Our rationality is not safe, if that is all we focus on, because it can disconnect us from our emotions, our intuitions, and our imagination. The institution is not safe either. The church, for instance, can become manipulative or strongly associated with the state. The Bible isn't safe either, if isolated from the other corners, because in order to understand reality fully we also need our reason, our experiences, and the institutions and traditions of the community to contextualize our reading of Scripture.

Sometimes people want to know, 'Which of the corners is most important? Which one takes precedence over the others?' But the four corners are not a hierarchy. No one is higher than another. They are a complementarity, meaning that all are necessary for understanding reality. There is no one corner that dominates all the others. They are not equal in function, nor are they interchangeable. They are all essential and distinct and unique. None of them are dependent, and none of them is first. They're all primary and all original.

Cheese or Beer: Which do you prefer?

People sometimes call the lecture which is the basis for this book the *Cheese Lecture*, because if you start with the **B** corner of the square, and move in a clockwise direction, the first letter of each corner spells *brie*, a French cheese. If you start in the **B** corner and move counter-clockwise, the letters almost spell *bier* in German. So you can have either beer or cheese. It is evidently a nutritious and inviting subject.

I once gave this talk in Switzerland, and an evangelical Bible scholar responded with the following comment: 'You need to redraw your diagram with the Bible on top, so that it trickles down over everything else, or else you need to put the Bible on the bottom, so it's the foundation of everything.' On a personal level as a pastor, I tended to agree with him. But I don't trust my natural tendency in this regard. Actually, I don't trust a lot of my natural tendencies. If I'm a sinner, if I'm broken and confused, if I'm distorted, then I should *expect* my view to be out of focus. That may not be an encouraging thing to say, but it's a real thing to say. I should expect my natural desires and tendencies and prejudices to be out of focus and out of kilter. So I have to make a deliberate effort to step back from my natural preferences, looking from a wider perspective than just myself. Only then do I start to see that all of the four corners are essential for a true and adequate epistemology.

Everybody has a favorite corner. We naturally feel that our strongest corner is the most true corner, and the corner that should govern all of the other corners. When we lean strongly enough toward one corner, we can develop an extremism or fanaticism. As a result, our epistemology becomes distorted and incomplete.

Stress, misunderstanding and confusion can arise when people favour one corner over another. Where do these preferences come from? Sometimes they're shaped by our personality and upbringing. Sometimes we inhale them from the cultural atmosphere in which we live. Sometimes preferences are inspired by our ignorance and blind spots. We may avoid or fear or downplay a corner because we don't know anything about it, or because we had a bad experience in that corner, or were manipulated in that corner, or suffered a failure or frustration in that corner—or because our Mom and Dad said negative things about that corner.

Sometimes, scientists discount the Bible because of their extreme emphasis on rationality. Christians may discount rationality because of their extreme emphasis on faith. It is only natural to want to strengthen what is strong, but we need to be careful about that natural tendency.

The apostle Paul was not afraid of his weaknesses. Before he was a Christian, while still a member of the Pharisee party, Paul was strong in a legalistic understanding of truth. After he became a Christian, various physical, social, and emotional experiences weakened his legalism, and consequently he developed a stronger and fuller epistemology. In his second letter to the Corinthians, Paul tells the reader, 'For when I am weak, then I am strong' (2 Corinthians 12:10). When Paul was strong in one corner, he was naturally strong. When this natural tendency became 'weaker', his epistemology became fuller and more spiritually strong—that is, more real and inclusive of the whole of reality.

Maybe we can think here of 'Judo' epistemology. 'Judo' is the 'gentle way', which gives way, falls back and uses an opposing force to shape reality. When we insist on the primacy of our favorite corner and are strong in it, our understanding of truth will be weak. When we fall back, and consider the surprising strength and validity of our non-favorite corners, our understanding of truth will be strengthened.

If we strengthen what is strong, we actually become weaker in our understanding of reality. If we strengthen what is weak, we become fuller, richer, and stronger in our epistemology. It's hard to accept this advice, because it requires humility, trust and faith—because we don't see the value of the weak things in life. We walk by sight in the area of strength, while we also need to walk by faith in the area that is weak. I find it exceedingly difficult to take that advice, and to actually deliberately strengthen what is weak. Approaching our weakness can make us feel quite vulnerable, and yet it is through this vulnerability that we can grow in our understanding and strength.

Preference in Religious Systems

The tendency to focus on a particular corner isn't only a problem with individuals. It happens in religious systems as a whole. The Bible corner can be overemphasized, to the exclusion of other corners, in evangelical forms of Christianity. The Bible can become the center of everything, marginalizing the importance of relationships, experience, and rationality. A similar overemphasis on a text can occur in certain forms of Judaism (Torah), Islam (Koran), and Mormonism (The Book of Mormon). In all of these instances, people may understand God and reality totally on the basis of a particular revelatory text. As I mentioned earlier, as an evangelical Christian I naturally tend to emphasize the **B** corner, but I have to be careful about that, and to avoid assuming that what I naturally prefer is the basic truth of human life.

In some worldviews, people tend to gravitate toward the rationality corner at the expense of the other three corners. Examples of such worldviews include atheistic humanism and communism. Both of these approaches tend to ignore or diminish human experience, and often try to work out the truth mathematically or scientifically. That is why, under the old communist regimes, writers and teachers were sometimes referred to as 'engineers of the human soul'.

Liberal branches of Christianity lean toward the rationality corner. Some liberal churches are hyper-intellectual, and will sift Bible content through an intellectual grid in order to shape it in a way that better fits the **R** corner. Many of these churches will attempt to strip away any supernatural or faith elements of Scripture and place them within the context of naturalistic explanations.

Great and exclusive strength in the rational corner can actually produce an epistemological weakness and incompleteness. Several years ago I was in Cluj-Napoca/Kolozsvár, the capital of Transylvania. A Christian café called Quo Vadis was having a series of open discussion evenings and I was invited to lead one. The Quo Vadis was decorated in early post-postmodern style and was one of the most interesting places in the city. About a dozen people gathered around a large, beautiful Art Nouveauish glass-topped table. Half of them were Christians and half were not. Their professions included teacher, nurse, psychologist, architect, historian and brain surgeon.

The Christians were the hosts and began the conversation with talk about the nature of faith, what to expect in answer to prayers, and experiences of the supernatural.

After about thirty minutes of this a man suddenly erupted in excellent English: 'Oh, you Christians with your experiences! I am a brain surgeon and can produce all your visions, emotions and sensations of what you call the supernatural surgically, electronically and chemically. There is no supernatural or God. There is only matter and energy in reality.' He went on with examples and illustrations for quite a while. I was listening and praying at the same time, asking for wisdom to answer this man. When he finally stopped, I surprised myself by saying, 'You speak as a man who has never been in love.' He froze and his face started to turn red. I asked, '*Are* you in love?' He said, 'Yes, I am.' I asked him, 'Can you reproduce your relationship with this woman in your laboratory and surgery—and does she know this?'

There was a long pause and then he said, 'You got me.' He was experiencing an epistemological paradigm shift. He saw the light. He could see that he could not reduce his experiences of life to matter and energy, but he wanted to reduce other peoples' experiences. He was a refreshingly honest and open person, and therefore probably an excellent scientist. He had been putting so much weight on the **R** or rationality corner that his epistemology was lopsided and distorted. The other three corners had been invalidated by his exclusive investment in the **R** corner. He seemed to be positive about broadening his epistemological base.

Other religious systems focus on the Institution corner. They overemphasize tradition, and are quite often nationalistic. Examples include certain versions of Shinto and Judaism. Within Christianity, Orthodox and Catholic churches may also tend toward the **I** or institution (tradition) corner. Protestants would tend to say that the Bible describes the church, and that in order to know what the church should be like, we need to begin with the Bible. They would have an epistemological hierarchy that looks like this:

God

Bible

Church

Orthodox believers believe the church wrote the Bible. Therefore, their epistemological hierarchy is:

God

Church

Bible

This means that the Bible must be understood within the Holy Tradition of Holy Mother Church.

Catholics tend toward an equal emphasis on Bible and Institution. They have a more open view of the revelatory activity of the Holy Spirit, in that they believe the Spirit continues to inspire the church. Catholics would have an epistemological hierarchy that looks something like this:

God

Bible + Church

I once spoke at the Gdansk Naval Academy in Poland, where all of the officer candidates were Catholic. They were on their feet shouting when I presented the four squares as all equal and necessary, because in their view I had insulted Holy Mother Church for not making Institution the foundation of all the other squares. I sympathized with their frustration, insofar as I agree that Institution is essential; it cannot be ignored or pushed into the background. But the other corners are also essential. If we say that any one corner is a derivative of one of the others, or a subsidiary of one of the others, then we will fight wars over which one is primary—and we *have* fought wars over which one is primary. But if we recognize that they are all essential, and their relationship is complementary rather than derivative or competitive, we will find a stability and peace and completeness.

Personal experience of reality is also an essential part of a full and healthy epistemology. However, some religious systems focus excessively on the experience corner. Examples include some forms of Hinduism and Buddhism, and New Age religions. Some forms of Pentecostal or charismatic Christianity also lean toward this corner. People in these kinds of churches sometimes understand the Bible not in terms of what it says, but in terms of how they experience what it says. This tendency would also be to some extent true of a postmodern reading of a text, in which the meaning of a text is the reader's response to the text.

Again, it is common that people tend to emphasize what comes naturally to them. A person with a sharp mind goes to the rationality corner, and might neglect or mistrust the experience corner. A person with strong life experiences might be drawn toward the experience corner, and be blessed by the experiences; they might then continue to move into this corner, to the point of neglecting or mistrusting the rationality corner—and then we would have the opposite problem. It's not a worse problem, it's just the opposite problem. This problem can and does occur in how people deal with all of the corners.

Your Epistemological Temperature

On your own, or with a group of people, consider the following questions about each of the four corners:

- What is your preferred corner for understanding truth?

- Does your personality play any role in this preference? For example, are you very emotional or in touch with your inner experiences? Or are you more rational and analytically minded?

- What aspect of truth was rewarded and encouraged when you were growing up?

- What aspect of truth was discouraged or punished?

- What aspect of truth was overlooked or ignored?

- What aspect of truth was considered dangerous?

- Currently, which corner or corners do you avoid or dislike?

- Which corner or corners do you try to control using your favorite corner?

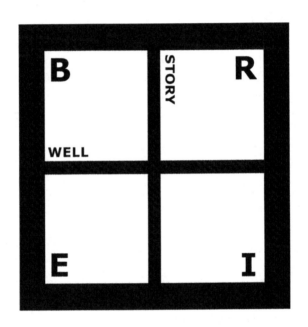

The Well and Story Approach

You may have noticed two axes across the center of our epistemology square—a horizontal line and a vertical line dividing up the square. These two axes will help us form an additional picture for understanding epistemology.

Let's name the two axes: we'll call one axis 'well' (like a water well) and the other axis 'story'. The well axis refers to a way of understanding revelatory texts, such as the Bible, Koran, or Torah. This approach involves drawing out what we need from a text, as we might draw water from a well. We put in our bucket and draw out data, guidance, comfort, inspiration, correction, rebuke, promises, and anything else that we might need. We know reality through actively engaging with it and experiencing its effect on us and our reaction to it.

In contrast, the story approach refers to a way of understanding that involves being aware of the overall frame of reality. This approach focuses on large historical sweeps of civilization or culture, or on the history of God's activity and intention as expressed in a text. The story approach places us and our experiences in the big picture, and allows us to know where we are and what we *mean*. This is perhaps a more passive approach of allowing the reality outside of ourselves to be what it is.

What is the center and focus of the well approach? It's me. What is the center and focus of the story approach? It's God or reality as a whole. People often wonder which of these two areas of focus matters more. They ask, 'Which is more important?' Can you see how wrong that question is? It's like somebody asking you which side of a coin you would like to have. You have to have both sides. A real coin that has value has two sides.

If the Bible is true, God made us to be significant people with subjective points of view. That means we should not only focus on God when reading the Bible, and pretend that we are irrelevant or don't exist. If God made us, then we must not discount ourselves. Our needs and our point of view matter.

However, if we just choose the well approach—ignoring the story approach—that makes experience our only teacher and disconnects us from the reality outside of ourselves. Without the context of the story approach, which is about God, we are alienated and isolated, because we are decontextualized from the whole of reality. The Bible is the story of God. It's the story of His character and activity in history. If we read the Bible without this framework, then we are not in a true relationship with God, who is greater than our subjective experience. Without this framework, there is no meaning in what we are reading—in fact, there is no meaning in anything—because meaning *means* relationships. Meaning, as I mentioned earlier, depends on a relationship to something outside of ourselves. Nothing has meaning in itself. If I isolate myself and only have the well approach, I have less and less meaning.

We are often confronted with questions that invite and challenge us to choose the well approach over the story approach, or the story approach over the well approach. But answering such questions can be destructive. We need both approaches in the same way that we need both sides of a coin to have a 'real' coin.

Let's put the well and story approaches into two columns, as shown below:

WELL	STORY

Now let's consider some contrasting pairs of words and ideas. We are going to place one of the pair under 'well' and the other under 'story'.

WELL	STORY
Subjective	Objective
Freedom	Form
Wife	Husband
Diversity	Unity
Mystery	Definition
Right-brain	Left-brain
Microscope	Telescope
Share my Faith	Share the Faith
My Testimony	Testimony of Jesus
Wave	Particle
Yin	Yang
Free Will	Predestination
Jesus as Man	Christ as God
Non-accurate Truth	Accurate Truth
Mercy	Justice
Educating	Teaching
Art	Science
Apophatic	Cataphatic
Deductive	Inductive
Grace	Law

In the chart to the left you see the elements of many pairs assigned to the 'well' or 'story' column. Look at each pair and reflect on it. What do you think? Do you think that any of the items is on the wrong side? Why? Some of the pairs may be more obvious than others. You may wish to share this exercise with other people, and see how they would place the items.

The first pair is 'subjective' and 'objective'. Most people can see that 'subjective', which relates to me or the viewer, goes in the well column; and that 'objective', which relates to that part of reality which is independent of me, goes in the story column. Following on from the complementarity of the four-cornered square, we see that the relationship between objective and subjective should not be competition but complementarity. Again, the question about choosing between them is destructive, because we need them both.

Now consider this pair: 'freedom' and 'form'. We can see that 'form' belongs in the story column, because it involves the general frame of reality. General forms would include, for instance, the laws of gravity and thermodynamics. On the other hand, 'freedom' belongs in the well column, and represents the infinite variety of choices and activity that are given meaning by the structure of the form. Again, both freedom and form are essential; they should not compete with each other.

The next pair is 'wife' and 'husband'. 'Wife' is more on the well side. The wife is a source (or well) of life. Life is born out of the wife. The wife is more like home, mother, comfort, intimacy, and unconditional acceptance. 'Husband' is more on the story side, because he provides a protecting context for the flourishing of the well. But which is more important in a marriage? The obvious answer is that they are equally important. But the relationship is not 50-50. If you take away the wife, you don't have 50% of a marriage left, because a marriage is 100% the wife. It is also 100% the husband. Marriage is a 200% reality—which is also true of our relationship with God. (Actually, a physicist has pointed out to me that the 100% of the wife is not added to the 100% of the husband, but multiplied by 100%. That would give us a 10,000% reality, making marriage a rich and complex thing indeed.)

The next pair is 'diversity' and 'unity'. What do you think? Into which column will you put each of them? Why? What about 'mystery' and 'definition'? Where will they go?

For each pair, which side is 'more true'? The answer is neither. Both are equally true, and both are needed for a full truth. For example, as we have said, both 'wife' and 'husband' are needed for the full truth of marriage. The two should not relate to each other in competition but in complementarity. This complementarity depends on the wife and husband being different from each other and not identical.

Let's take a closer look at another pair. Consider the pair 'my faith' and 'the faith'. In many Christian groups one mostly hears about sharing 'my faith', but not much about sharing 'the faith'. In order to bring this pair into a whole and balanced focus, I like to ask people the question, 'Who is Jesus Christ before you were born?' This question is difficult for people who concentrate on the well approach to reality. They know how they feel about Jesus, and what they have experienced of Jesus in their own lives; but they might not have learned much, through the story approach, about who Jesus is independent of their experiences. They can speak more about their unique experiences of Jesus than they can about the objective reality of Jesus—which can actually be shared. It is more possible to share 'the faith' than 'my faith'. We all share and know together the facts about Jesus; our experiences of Jesus are more private and more difficult to share.

On the other hand, there are people who know a great deal about Jesus but don't have any actual experience with Jesus. This leans too far on the story side and doesn't make a complete reality either.

Notice that some parts of reality don't fit in the well and story columns. 'Good' and 'evil' are not presented as a pair because, in the biblical worldview, good and evil are not two complementary aspects of truth or equal opposites. Good is the original reality; evil is a derivative distortion. Only good is true; evil is false. This view is in contrast with dualistic worldviews, in which 'good' and 'evil' are both regarded as equally original in reality, and equally important in comprising truth.

For the same reason, the columns do not include the pairs 'love' and 'hate', or 'light' and 'darkness'—because, again, only the first member of each pair is true and original.

Finally, consider 'impersonal' and 'personal'. Do we exist in a reality that is fundamentally material and energetic with personal configurations—or a reality that is fundamentally personal, functioning in and out of a material and energetic matrix? If the Bible is true, then reality is fundamentally personal rather than mechanical or energetic. That is why the columns do not include the pair 'personal' and 'impersonal'; only 'personal' is true.

Seeing with a Single Eye

In our exploration of the four epistemology corners, we saw that people tend to have a favorite corner. The same is true of the well and story columns. People who value experiences will probably prefer the well column, whereas people who value reason and rationality will probably emphasize the story column. Most of us will have a natural tendency for one column over the other. Again, my advice is to strengthen what is weak, and bring a balance and wholeness into your approach to reality.

As we pray and work on strengthening our weaknesses, we will begin to see reality in a way that is more whole and complete. We will begin to experience a fuller living knowledge, rather than a partial knowledge. The process will be challenging and at times frightening, because it will involve a paradigm shift, or change in our model of reality. It will take us out of our comfort zone.

In the Sermon on the Mount, there is a little section where Jesus teaches about two areas of conflict in human life: investing and serving. He says (Matthew 6:19-21, 24):

Do not store up for yourselves treasures on earth, where moths and vermin destroy, and where thieves break in and steal. But store up for yourselves treasures in heaven, where moths and vermin do not destroy, and where thieves do not break in and steal. For where your treasure is, there your heart will be also...No one can serve two masters. Either you will hate the one and love the other,

or you will be devoted to the one and despise the other.
You cannot serve both God and money.

We are encouraged to invest ourselves in the total reality of heaven, which includes the earth, rather than investing in the limited, isolated and unviable context of the creation alone. We are encouraged to serve the Giver and not the gifts. We need to serve the God who gives the capacity to produce wealth. In between these two areas of (apparent) conflict is a little and much misunderstood section about perspective. Jesus says (Matthew 6:22-23):

The eye is the lamp of the body. If your eyes are healthy,
your whole body will be full of light. But if your eyes are
unhealthy, your whole body will be full of darkness. If
then the light within you is darkness, how great is that
darkness!

Our perception (the eye) is the light source of our life. Most modern translations render verse 22 as 'if your eye is good' or 'sound' or 'healthy', but the original Greek word is 'single'. This means to have a united, comprehensive and complimentary view of reality as a whole. In this way the apparent conflicts of the surrounding sections about investment and service are resolved. When we see 'storing up' and 'serving' in this single way or with a 'holistic' focus, then the conflicts are resolved by contextualizing everything in the Kingdom of God. We experience producing wealth and serving people as part of our lives in God's Kingdom. Can you see a connection between this section of the Sermon on the Mount and the four corners of our epistemology square, and the two axes? If we hold the four corners and two columns in complementary focus, will we be more full of light?

Seeing with a 'single' eye can be challenging. It means bringing together aspects of reality that don't seem to fit together rationally. Rationality is important, but it can be overemphasized and cause distortions—even in the church. During the Enlightenment and the scientific revolution, when there emerged a strong faith that all truth can be expressed in numbers, people began to draw reality on flat surfaces, using circle graphs and bar graphs. All the divisions always added up to 100%.

The Bible doesn't divide things up that way, but even the church took on the principles of the world and began to try to understand truth through the world's glasses. As a result, Christians have tended to divide everything up in mathematical terms. For example, the reality of predestination and free will is sometimes laid out on a flat surface as a pie chart, and people try to divide the pie into parts that add up to 100%. Some people divide the pie into 50-50 halves, but that doesn't seem very honouring to God's sovereignty. Other people might say that the pie is divided into 51% God's sovereignty and 49% people's free will. This is also not satisfactory. Even if we say it should be divided into 99% God's sovereignty and 1% free will, it still does not satisfy. The most logical understanding is that God is 100% sovereign—which means that human beings are chess pieces—or that human free will is 100% free—which means that God is on a deistic holiday.

It seems to me that instead of squashing reality onto a two-dimensional pie chart, it might be better to think of a free will disc, and predestination disc. Both the free will disc and the predestination disc are 100%. The discs interface to form a three-dimensional sphere of reality. This sphere expresses a 200% reality—or, as I mentioned earlier, a 10,000% reality. God's sovereignty is total and complete, and human free will is total and complete. The relationship between the sovereignty of God and the free will of man is not competition if we see them as a three-dimensional model rather than a two-dimensional model.

Just as we must see predestination and free will with a 'single eye', we must also see other seeming divisions, differences, and contrasts as unified. When we read the Bible, the well approach and the story approach are both necessary to understanding the truth. If we want to understand God and absolute reality in the fullest way, we

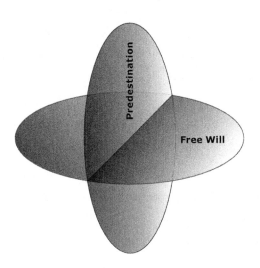

need to bring together all the major sources of this understanding, including the Bible, our experiences, rationality, and institutions or tradition. None of these stands above the others, and none of them can be left out.

The fact is that we are all unbalanced. We are all unhealthy. So the question is not, 'Am I unbalanced?' The question is, 'How am I unbalanced? How can I be healed?' We need to approach these challenges with humility.

Humility is not shyness or obsequiousness. Humility is realism. When I am realistic, I realize both my strengths and my weaknesses accurately. If I have a God-given strength for teaching, and I say, 'No, I'm sure I couldn't do that. I'm sure others could do it better'—that is not humility, it is pride. It is saying, 'God has made me with this strength, but I would feel better and people would think more highly of me, if I would deny it.' This looks like humility, but it isn't. It is creating myself according to the vanity of my own imagination. Real humility is accepting ourselves as we actually are, and not pretending to be strong or weak in ways that seem convenient to us.

Can we look at ourselves closely, and see our areas of distortion? Can we face our areas of distortion honestly, and through work and faith build a more comprehensive approach to our understanding of reality? It can take some effort. It makes life more complicated, and leaves us more vulnerable. But a complementary approach to truth makes our lives richer and fuller. It grounds us in reality and brings us into greater wholeness.   Amen.

33 QUESTIONS

These questions are taken from recordings of actual Q&A sessions after lectures and from readers of the lecture text. They have been only minimally edited, and therefore have a conversational rather than an academic or literary tone.

A real question helps us stop fluttering around a subject like moths and get to the heart of things. Only an ignorant question is a true question. It can be harder to ask good questions than to give good answers. What are your questions? Invest yourself in finding them.

1. *What are some of the obstacles that people face as they explore the Bible corner of epistemology?*

One obstacle is that people feel hurried. Sometimes Christians urge people to make a decision about the authority of the Bible without giving them time to think it through. People can feel pressure to understand everything about the Bible before they accept it as an authoritative source. Actually, we never understand any of the four sources fully. The Bible is perfect, but our understanding of it never is. So we shouldn't put pressure on ourselves to have a perfect understanding. People who believe that they have a perfect understanding of the Bible, or of any of the other sources of knowledge, sometimes become dangerous. My advice is to slow down. The search for truth is a *process* and it takes time.

Another common obstacle is that people are reluctant to accept the truth of the Christian faith unless they can prove that everything else is totally false. But I don't think that reflects reality. Buddhism doesn't need to be proven totally false in order for you to choose Jesus. Islam doesn't need to be proven totally false in order for you to be saved as a Christian. Other worldviews include some elements of truth, even if the worldviews as a whole don't adequately represent the absolute truth.

People also expect the Bible to be what it is not, and this too can be an obstacle. The Bible is not a science textbook, although what it says about reality does not conflict with science. Similarly, the Bible was written in other times and cultures, and sometimes people mistakenly expect it to speak directly to our time and culture in our terms.

2. People with authority easily confuse having authority with having more worth and value. 'I've got the power, so I'm more important and superior.' Can you comment on this?

Within God, the Father has authority and gives it to the Son; the Father commands and sends, and the Son obeys and goes. They are equally God. The same applies to the image of God—human beings. For example, parents have authority and children obey, but who is more human? They are both equally human. Having authority does not humanize a person, but rather has a specific function within human relationships.

Years ago, I was in communist East Germany in a church with about a hundred people. Most of them were farmers. I asked, 'Who is more human, the parents or the children?' They all said, 'The parents.' I was so shocked that I could barely catch my breath. I didn't know what to say. They were sure of their answer. There was no discussion. There was no speculation. That was reality for them. The parents were more human, the children were less human. And I thought to myself, 'I'm in a different culture now. I'm out of my box. How do I cope with this? What do I do?' I just had to move on. And these were Christians. I would call them, in my own egocentric way, Bible-believing Christians, but not Bible-understanding

Christians. They accepted the authority of the Bible as I do, and we were brothers, but I think they misunderstood something important. Fundamentally, we were together, but there were some ways that we were quite different.

Life is complex, even among Christians. We cannot expect all Christians to have the same cultural, political, economic, and social values and structures. Sometimes we will find ourselves in a culture, and our gut reaction will be, 'Oh, that's abnormal!'

But the real question is, 'Is it abnormal to God, or is it only abnormal to me?' If it's only abnormal to me, then I need to accept it. But if it's abnormal to God, if it's really outside His character and commands and the structure He gives for human life, then I need to say, 'There's a problem here. You're making a mistake, dear brother, and I feel called to persuade you of that.' But we have to be careful and humble, and really look to see whether we are speaking from cultural prejudice, or from a godly perspective.

3. *Can people under authority get confused about how to function in a relationship of authority?*

Sometimes people under authority want people with authority to take far more responsibility for their lives than they should. It can be very relaxing not to be responsible for your own life, and comforting to be dependent on others. But that would be a confused and wrong use of authority.

People under authority are sometimes victims. We tend to think of victims as innocent. In some ways, of course, they are, particularly in specific areas of victimization. But victims are people, and all people are guilty. No one should be reduced to being only a victim. Some people can manipulate reality through their victim status. Some feel that the meaning of life is to discover what life owes them, and to devote themselves to collecting. This is not how life actually works.

I often say, 'Without guilt there is no hope.' If we are only innocent victims, then all of our problems are caused by bad things that happen to us. In this case, the only hope is that better things will happen to us. But no one is promising us that better things will happen. If we are guilty, we need to be forgiven, and Someone is promising forgiveness.

4. *Can you talk more about how freedom and form relate to authority?*

I'll use the example of parents again. The authority of parents shapes the freedom of young children. Parents impose constraints in some areas of a child's life, but not in others. 'You can do *this*,' parents often say, 'but you can't do *that*.' Parents shape freedom in this way so that the children can live, safely and fully; in other words, the freedom that parents offer is a freedom that has form. It's not a shifting cloud of freedom, or a willy-nilly kind of freedom. A freedom without form is dangerous.

I offer you an equation:

$$\text{Total freedom} = \text{Death}$$

That's a politically incorrect statement in a postmodern culture, where the highest value is freedom, but it seems to me it's quite true. If you give your children total freedom, they will not survive. They will die. If a society tries to live in total freedom, without any form of marriage, family, traffic laws, regulations for what medications are sold, and so on, we won't survive very long. But if there is no freedom, then there is paralysis. That's not a good way to live, either. So freedom is essential for life, but it must be in a complementary relationship with form.

What we tend to do is swing like a pendulum between form and freedom in various sizes of swings. We have historical swings that take centuries, and we have societal swings that can be more rapid, and we have personal swings that can happen several times an hour. I may crave the form, and the security of the form, and then I may move over to the freedom—and often I can't find a good balance between the two. There's always a tension, a struggle, an imbalance. There's always an overemphasis, an incompleteness, a lack of focus in the relationship between form and freedom. There's too much of one or too much of the other. I might have excessive form in my academic life, and excessive freedom in my sexual life, or my friendship life, or my social life. It's difficult to get the whole picture stabilized *and* dynamic. If it's only stable and not dynamic, it's dead, and if it's only dynamic and not stable, it's chaos. How do we get the picture right with dynamic stability? Getting back to your question, a good authority will describe reality in a way that strikes the right balance between freedom *and* form. A bad authority, or a distorted or misused authority, will end up being too extreme one way or the other—allowing too much freedom with no proper form, or too much form and regulation with no proper freedom.

5. What if I don't like the authority of a particular institution? What if it doesn't seem rational?
What if, in the case of traffic lights, it's arguably more rational to make green mean stop and red mean go?

It may indeed seem more rational to some people. But knowledge is more than rational. It involves love, humility, submission, cooperation and service. All of these things occur among God, within the relationships of the Trinity. If we are made in God's image, then those elements should be a part of our way of living. To be able to submit is a powerful and humanizing thing—a reality which our contemporary Western culture doesn't know.

Our culture overemphasizes the individual. It overemphasizes personal power and personal achievement. But if we have no capacity for submission, then we'll have problems. We'll lack humility, and service, and cooperation. Although I may agree that it seems more rational for green to mean stop and red to mean go in a traffic light, I also need to balance my rational preference with the authority of tradition, and to submit to that tradition.

The same is true in many other matters in life: sometimes I need to submit.

The first book of Peter tells us that we should submit for the sake of God, not because our government or rulers are perfect, but because God is perfect and He has asked us to do so. Peter also says you should submit to your master (or 'employer' in modern terms). Most of the English translations say that we should submit even if the master is 'harsh', but the actual correct word is *skolios*, which means 'twisted' and even 'crooked'. It means that you should submit to the authority of your master even if he's a dubious character, because the authority is given by God and the master's character is incidental. Of course there is room for other considerations, but the point is, it's stated quite strongly, and so we need to work with that reality.

6. How do we know that we can trust God?

We can trust God because He loves us. But how do we know He loves us? That's complicated. We may be taught that it's true, but there is no formula to demonstrate it. The only way to know God is as a living and personal reality. Entering into that reality can be unsettling, because we don't know what to expect.

It's as if you're starving, and you've been offered a bowl of soup, but at the last moment before putting the spoon to your lips, you wonder, 'Is this soup healthy or poisoned?' That's a reasonable question, and there are various ways of finding out the answer. You can interview the cook and see if he's a homicidal maniac. You can wait for others to eat the soup and watch to see if anyone falls over. If you're very bright, you may decide to chemically analyze the soup—although even a chemical analysis may not give you a clear answer, because the soup may react differently in your metabolism, or its properties may change in the cooling process. There are all sorts of variables, but none of them will be sufficient to give you the answer. The only way to really know if the soup is good for you is to eat it. That's living by faith. We eat by faith or we starve to death. Knowledge and reasoning can be helpful, and can inform faith, but they will only take us so far. Faith is necessary.

The Bible tells us *taste and see that the Lord is good.* Normally when we taste we don't see, and when we see we don't taste. God is combining our senses in a holistic way in this statement. Knowing that we can trust God cannot be reduced to one sense. It cannot be reduced to thinking, tasting, seeing, or feeling, but needs to combine all of these and more. On top of all of this, we need to add faith, in order to complete our knowledge that God is trustworthy. We come to God with our whole being.

7. Does the Holy Spirit help us to know through our feelings?

Yes, but sometimes what we feel in our hearts can *seem* like the Holy Spirit, when it actually isn't—and in these situations our feelings can contradict the Bible. In my work as a pastor, a woman once came to me and said, 'The Holy Spirit has told me to leave my husband and serve the Lord as a missionary.' I explored the woman's feelings and her situation, which of course wasn't enough. We also explored what the Bible says about the marital relationship, and it was only because of the Bible that I was able to tell her that it wasn't the Holy Spirit guiding her. Although our personal experience is important, there will be situations when, as we put our experience together with what the Bible says, it turns out that our experience is misleading.

8. Can people misinterpret their own experiences by misreading the Bible?

That does happen sometimes. For example, people may believe that they love God, when they actually don't, because they have failed to understand what the Bible says about love. The Bible is clear that there's only one way to know that we love God, and that is that we love other people. In other words, we have two different kinds of experiences—the experience of loving God, and the experience of loving other people—and these two experiences must go together. Another way of saying this is that the experience of loving God must be incarnational as well as transcendental. If we have the emotion of loving God, it might be only transcendental; it might be only an idea or feeling that we assume to be connected to the supernatural, but which has no physical practical evidence. The true test of whether our love for God is an actual spiritual experience is whether we love other people. This incarnational experience validates our transcendental experience of loving God; these two experiences happen together in a complementary relationship.

We see a similar dynamic when it comes to faith and works. The apostle James tells us, 'Show me your faith without deeds, and I will show you my faith by my deeds...faith without deeds is dead.' The relationship between faith and works is complementary. We know that we have one when we have the other; if we don't have both, then we don't really have either. People who read the Bible sometimes don't grasp this essential point, and may believe that they have faith based only on a feeling, or based only on activities.

9. Would it be fair to say that you have mixed feelings about postmodernism?

I certainly do. I am grateful for postmodernism because it has restored subjectivity to truth. I am unhappy with postmodernism because it has eliminated objectivity from truth.

10. *Can 'well and story' be applied to experience, rationality, and institution?*

Yes. On the well side of the **I** corner, we may experience our church, or nation, or ethnic associations, or other communities, in terms of our identity, security, and motivation. On the story side of the **I** corner, we may see the whole picture of an institution or of a community, including its history, and where we might fit into that picture. So, on the well side, we may experience pride and encouragement as part of our ethnicity; whereas on the story side, we may see ourselves in the context of the overall community, and understand our role and contributions within this overall frame.

The **E** corner can also be seen in both well and story terms. On the well side, we may experience excitement, or joy, or peace, through experiences such as singing songs, or walking in nature, or skiing. On the story side, we may see our experiences within the overall frame of our lives over time, and understand these experiences in relation to one another. The story side of the **E** corner may overlap somewhat with the **I** corner.

The **R** corner can similarly be understood in well and story terms. On the well side, we may experience curiosity, excitement, and satisfaction, when we explore and learn new things based on reason. Scientists and engineers can probably relate to such experiences. On the story side, we may see how the things we have learned or discovered are related to other areas of knowledge and the historical progression of science. For instance, if I am an aviation engineer and have invented a new type of aircraft, then I may see how this aircraft emerged from earlier models, and how it fits within the progress of aviation history.

11. *How did you arrive at your four epistemological corners? What persuaded you that these corners are a full frame of knowledge?*

The four corners themselves are behind my epistemology. As I've gone through life, I have tried to be rational, and I have seen how reason can help us understand the world. I have lived in various traditions, such as being part of a nation or family, and so I see that such traditions are an important part of understanding reality. I have had personal experiences of great strength, and it seems that they too need to be integrated into knowledge. My life has also been informed by revelation, and that also needs a place. I am always and constantly struggling to integrate these four corners. It never works perfectly. I have to trust God, especially when I can't fully figure it out for myself—which is always. In fact, if I *could* figure it all out for myself, I would not need God, and I would become a humanistic atheist. This is actually what happened to Eve in the Garden of Eden in her encounter with the serpent and the fruit of the knowledge of good and evil. The serpent said to Eve that she would become like God if she ate the fruit and came to know for herself. This is the situation for all of us; we're all eating the fruit, we're all claiming knowledge that makes us independent of God.

74

12. *Sometimes scientists and pastors disagree on things like the age of the Earth, because they're coming from different corners. What suggestions would you have to encourage a better dialogue in situations like this?*

I would suggest a certain amount of humility. The corners need to be kept together, and seen in complementary relationships. The Bible should not be read in isolation; it was not written for the angels, but for human beings who live in space-time and history, which includes the rational progression of scientific investigation. We have to be careful and not expect the various corners to speak each other's language. The rationality corner is going to be committed to speaking as objectively as possible; but the Bible, being a personal communication, includes subjectivity. For instance, the parables of Jesus are true, and their truth is not confined to objective fact. They are not objectively accurate, but they are true.

13. *Your statement 'not objectively accurate' brings to mind the distinction between 'accurate' and 'non-accurate' truth that you made in your book,* 3 THEORIES OF EVERYTHING. *This distinction is shown in the 'well and story' columns of the present volume. Can you elaborate on this?*

Allow me to give you an example that I often share with people. If you want to build a true bridge, then you need to approach the project objectively. You need to make exact mathematical calculations. If you do so, then you will be able to build an objectively accurate bridge.

On the other hand, you cannot fall in love accurately. The experience is subjective, with chaotic and unpredictable emotions. You cannot plan the process of falling in love. However, you would not say that falling in love is not true because it is subjective. It is very true—just ask anybody who has fallen in love—but true in a non-accurate way. The objectivity of the bridge is the same for everybody, but the subjectivity of falling in love is unique and exclusive. A more complete experience of truth might be falling in love on a bridge.

14. *Are there only four corners? Are there any more?*

There could be more sources, but I think those four cover most of life. While giving lectures on epistemology, a few people have suggested additional corners, but after some consideration it always turned out that the new corners could be subsumed under the four existing corners.

15. *What you teach about the objective aspect of truth implies definitions of some things. People are often uncomfortable with definitions. Why is that?*

Sometimes people, especially postmodern people, are afraid of definitions, because they fear that definitions will paralyze them. People think of definitions as a point that doesn't move. But a definition is not a point, it's a circle, and in a circle there are infinite points. If I ask Silvio to bring me a cup of tea and he comes back with it, it might be mint tea in a mug, black tea in a cup and saucer, tea with lemon, tea with milk, tea with honey, plant tea, Earl Grey tea, or jasmine tea. There are an infinite number of things that it could be, but it will not be a hammer, because hammer is outside the circle of 'cup of tea'. So is *banana*. So is *chair*. Definition is essential for my life, because if I don't have the definition, I will have to drink a hammer and I will die. In other words, it's life and death to have definitions. Definitions have an authority over meaning, and we need that authority. It isn't a matter of how we feel about it. If someone makes tea for you and puts poison in it, whether you die or not is not a question of whether you have *given* authority to the poison to kill you. The poison has authority whether you give it or not.

Where does authority come from? The Bible tells us that 'All authority comes from God.' That's either true or it's not true. If it is true, then we need to remain and work within that understanding. It doesn't mean that authority is properly used by people, and it doesn't mean we will always like it. It only means it comes from God, because there is authority in and among God. Therefore, we cannot live without authority. We have to have things outside of us that describe reality for us. We can't invent reality for ourselves. Postmodern people move strongly in that direction, of inventing reality for themselves, but I don't think they are really able to do it. I think we all live in a reality that is independent of our attitude.

16. *Some branches of the Protestant church have become very liberal and very critical towards the Bible. Can you comment on this trend?*

This trend is a result of the Enlightenment and scientism becoming the salt and light of the church, by demanding that the Bible's truth be only objective. Many Christians have absorbed this rationalistic expectation. When the Bible doesn't conform to this expectation, liberal Christians can become insecure and abandon the truth of the Bible. On the other hand, fundamentalist Christians can be forced into a corner and try to make the Bible speak only objectively.

17. *How much clarity should we expect when reading the Bible?*

We should expect a great deal of clarity. However, if you demand perfect clarity from your Bible, then the **R** corner is probably dictating how you read it. You are probably interpreting it through very rationalistic glasses. An extreme example of this tendency would be somebody doing research to determine the identity of the mother of the prodigal son. Another example would be trying to identify the precise correspondence of all the images in the parables, and to distill from the parables specific instructions and prescriptions for life. A better way to approach the parables is as windows that Jesus opened, through which we all see reality from different points of view. As I suggested earlier, the parables are an example of non-accurate truth. A further example of non-accurate truth would be the passage in John, chapter 6: 'Whoever eats my flesh and drinks my blood remains in me, and I in them.' This passage is true, but does not lend itself to an 'accurate' scientific reading.

18. *Some people who want to be strong in their Christian faith may stick to the* **B** *corner and avoid the other three corners, fearing the other three corners might cause uncertainty in their faith. Any thoughts about this?*

I think Christians should consider the possibility that faith in the Bible is strengthened by contextualizing it with the other three corners. We can't go and live inside the Bible; the Bible helps us to live in the world. We don't need to be afraid of any of the corners, although they all have their dangers. None of the corners is safe. The devil tried to distort even Jesus' reading of the Bible (as we see in Luke 4: 9-11)—so not even the Bible corner is completely safe. We shouldn't get too comfortable and fall asleep in any of the corners.

19. *Is it possible for the* **R** *corner to support the* **B** *corner?*

Yes. The **R** corner is the basis for historical and archeological research. During the eighteenth century, many scholars believed that writing had not yet been invented during the time of Moses, meaning that the early books of the Bible must not have been written at the time they are claimed to have been written. However, during the nineteenth century archeologists discovered the Code of Hammurabi, which was written around 1700 B.C. The discovery that people were already writing before Moses gave strength to the view that the early books of the Bible could have been written around the time of the events described in these books.

20. Christians often want to submit to the Bible. Should we also submit to the other three corners?

The authorities of all the four corners need to be contextualized with each other, in a complementary rather than a competitive way. We shouldn't submit to any of the corners in isolation, because that would be a form of idolatry. It's taking only a part of reality and absolutizing it. We may find ourselves worshipping the Bible, or experience, or tradition, or rationality, and end up with distortions of our understanding of reality. Remember that each corner is essential.

21. Some people might argue that we can do fine with just the E, I, and R corners, leaving out the B corner. Are there any risks in doing this?

There are various risks. One is that, if there is a supernatural reality, then only using the **E**, **I**, and **R** corners, without the **B** corner, would leave you open to an awareness of the supernatural, without any guide. Many people say 'I am spiritual but not religious', meaning that they're aware of the supernatural, but they don't have any way to integrate it into the **E**, **I**, and **R** corners. It makes their spirituality highly subjective and unstable. Without the Bible, it's difficult to have any objective aspects to spirituality.

Another risk is that with only the **E**, **I**, and **R** corners, people are working within a humanistic relativism. People need absolutes if they are made in the image of God, who *is* absolute. In a postmodern culture, people are wary of absolutes, and like to think that there aren't any. At conferences where I've lectured, the organizers have made T-shirts that read, 'Are all absolutes absurd?' This question eats itself by the tail, because if all absolutes are absolutely absurd, then so is this one. The only escape from absurdity is to have absolutes, which the **B** corner gives us.

22. *Is there no way to establish an absolute from the objective nature of the* **R** *corner?*

One could arrive at an absolute, but it would be mechanical and impersonal. We humans experience a life that includes the subjective and the personal, so we would not fit or belong in a totally rational or objective absolute.

23. *Muslims and Hindus might take the Bible out of the* **B** *corner and insert some other special revelation or spiritual text, such as the Koran or Vedas.*
How can we know if that version of epistemology is more or less valid than one in which the Bible is in the Revelation corner?

We need to examine the suggested revelatory texts, and see if they fit history and science, and life as we live it. We need to be careful not to approach these texts religiously, by worshipping them or making assumptions that they're true, but by asking questions about them. We should examine the Revelation text (or **B** corner) to see if it complements the other three corners, or if it contradicts them. In my view, the Bible belongs with the other three corners better than any other revelatory text.

24. *Your epistemological framework implicitly recognizes the role of science, which relies heavily on reason. Does art also inform our epistemology?*

Art, or creativity, functions largely in the **E** corner. Art helps us to experience reality and to organize experience in a variety of ways. We should include in art literature, drama, poetry, dance, cooking, conversation, music, sculpting, interior decorating, clothes design, architecture, and of course painting. Good artists want to help people know reality more fully. A principal contribution of artists to epistemology is to show in some way that one thing is like another. The artist says, 'This is like that' and everyone else says, 'Oh, so it is! I never saw that before.' Art can be true or false or helpful or unhelpful, and therefore must always be tested to see if it relates in a complementary manner with the other three corners.

25. You mentioned that authority functions best when there is trust. Can you say more about trust, and other elements that are important in relationships of authority?

Relationships of authority do need trust in order to function at their best. When there is no trust, the stance of the person under authority will be one of avoidance, subversion, or rebellion toward the person or institution that has authority. Faithfulness and consistency are also important in authority, as well as respect. For instance, the person who has authority must respect the person who is under authority. Respecting means recognizing that the person under authority has the same value as the person with authority, even though he or she has a different role.

On that note, we also need to have a clear awareness of our role and place in a relationship of authority. As I mentioned earlier, humility is realism. It isn't a matter of what we want or feel like, nor a policy of always being a doormat. It is a matter of being honestly aware of the real situation and condition in which we are.

Sometimes we need the humility to accept that we are *under* authority. Sometimes we need the humility to accept that we *have* authority. Both can be difficult. If we don't accept these realities, we have misunderstanding, confusion, and possibly conflict. Although authority is essential for life, it can often be destructive so we need to be wise and careful about it.

26. You said that gravity has authority. But if authority is the 'power to describe reality,' in what sense does gravity 'describe' reality? Gravity doesn't talk.

Talking isn't the only way to communicate or demonstrate something. Gravity 'tells' us that if we jump off a tall building we will be hurt. It's important to listen to this message and take it seriously. 'Describe' means to scribe a line or circle around something and make it defined and distinct from other parts of reality. Gravity draws a line around walking, for instance, and puts it on the ground instead of on the ceiling or in the air.

27. Has anybody else devised a four-corner epistemological model like yours?

Yes, John Wesley developed what is called the 'Wesleyan Quadrilateral', which involves four sources of authority for theological reflection. Wesley's four sources, like mine, are Scripture, tradition, experience, and reason. However, the purpose of his Quadrilateral method is theological reflection, whereas my purpose is epistemology. I discovered Wesley's work after I had finished working mine out and was pleased to be in his company.

28. *You often talk about 'reality'. What do you mean by 'reality'?*

Reality is who God is, what He does, and what He wants. That means that evil is unreal, and sin is unreal. God made us to be real, and when we choose to live in unreality, He gets very upset.

When I say 'real', I mean total, comprehensive, absolute Reality, and not some aspect or experience of reality. The same would apply to 'truth'. Truth with a capital T is basically the same as Reality. Truth must include love, because love is part of who God is, what He does, and what He wants.

29. *Before the Bible came into being, could anybody have had a complete epistemology? Similarly, today there may be places and cultures in the world where people have not yet been exposed to the Bible.*
Is it possible for such people to experience a complete epistemology?

No one experiences a complete epistemology except God as a Trinity. However, it would certainly be possible for the people in your question to have an epistemology that is adequate for salvation. The first corner, as I've noted earlier, is actually 'Revelation' as well as 'Bible'. That is, God gives us revelation not only through the Bible, but through the creation as a whole, the uniqueness of human beings, and direct revelation. The working of the Holy Spirit is not limited to the Bible; He reveals truth to people through dreams, observations of nature and other ways. God has put eternity in the hearts of all people. The question is how we respond to Him. A 'saving' epistemology must also include faith, whether a person has a Bible in his hand or not.

30. *You mentioned that 'Revelation means information that comes from the supernatural into the natural world.' Can you say a little more about the differences between the supernatural and natural world?*

The natural world, which is created, includes Earth and the physical universe, and is the subject of scientific investigation. The supernatural world, which is also created, includes angels and demons. There is also the supernatural world which is *uncreated*; this refers to God himself, who was not created but has always existed. The supernatural world (both created and uncreated) cannot be fully accessed scientifically, because it exists and functions partly in dimensions that are unavailable to physical investigation.

31. *People say that 'Seeing is believing'. What do you think about that?*

I think it is true. Seeing is believing—but also believing is seeing. For example, because we believe that someone loves us or is trustworthy, we see them differently. We don't only believe because we see; believing changes the *way* we see. When belief changes how we see, it doesn't necessarily make us see more truly, or less truly. Belief needs to be tested by what we see. Seeing and believing belong together. They should work together in a complementary relationship for a full epistemology.

32. *The four corners, and well and story, inform our understanding of reality as a whole. But how do people apply them to their everyday lives? In what areas of ordinary, everyday life can you see an application of the four corners, or the well and story?*

The corners and columns keep us from being unbalanced in our thinking and expectations of life. For example, in the case of marriage, using the corners, and well and story, can help people realize that marriage is not more 'male' or more 'female'. Another example would involve reading texts. We know the meaning of a text in various ways—for instance, by what it says and how I respond to it. Using the corners and columns helps us to keep those ways of knowing in complementarity.

A third example would involve raising children. In this case, the corners and columns help us to keep children within the objective aspect of reality, rather than in a complete fantasy reality; at the same time, it allows them their subjective experience of reality.

33. Can we know if someone is saved?

Salvation means changing from a self-centered, dead condition, to an other-centered living condition by the power of Jesus. Salvation is a fact that has an effect. The Bible speaks of salvation and the assurance of salvation, which are not exactly the same thing. If someone is religious, and has had religious experiences, and does not grow in the fruits of the Spirit (love, joy, peace, patience, kindness, goodness, faithfulness, gentleness, and self-control) there is no evidence or assurance that the person actually belongs to God and has new life in Christ. In such a situation there are two possibilities; either the person was never saved, and there is no new life (this is probably the safest assumption), or the person is saved and having a really rough time. Human beings are not the Holy Spirit, so our epistemology is limited.

Some things only God knows for sure.

Ellis Potter after a lecture in 2015
Glasgow School of Art

Many thanks to

Peco Gaskovski
for his patient editing and persistent
motivation.

Katharine Wolff
for making this book intelligently
beautiful while developing guidelines
for the trilogy.

Marsh Moyle
for his careful reading and generously
insightful comments on the text.

Ruth Gaskovski
for her inspiring encouragement and for
transcribing the original recordings.

Destinée Media aims to bring a fresh perspective to living, culture, and worldviews. This is the second book of a trilogy based on the lectures of Ellis Potter.

CPSIA information can be obtained
at www.ICGtesting.com
Printed in the USA
LVOW03s0207281117
557718LV00019BA/787/P